I'll Find You Again

Cornell Hurley Jr. and Shirley Ann Thomas

I'll Find You Again:
A True Love Story

By Cornell Hurley Jr.
And
Shirley Thomas

Cadmuspublishing.com

I'LL FIND YOU AGAIN:
A TRUE LOVE STORY

Manufactured in the United States of America. Copyright 2024 by Cornell Hurley Jr and Shirley Thomas. All rights reserved. No part of this book may be reproduced in any form, audio, digital, or in print, except excerpts by reviewers, without written permission from the copyright holder or Cadmus Publishing LLC.

DISCLAIMER:

The thoughts, opinions, and expressions herein are those of the author and do not reflect those of Cadmus Publishing LLC. Any similarities to actual events or people are purely coincidental. Names and distinguishing characteristics may have been changed to preserve the identities of any individuals. Published by Cadmus Publishing LLC. P. O. Box 8664. Haledon, NJ 07538
Web: Cadmuspublishing.com
Web: Booksbyprisoners.com
Web: MusicbyPrisoners.com
Facebook.com/Cadmuspublishing
Business email: admin@cadmuspublishing.com
Author email: info@cadmuspublishing.com
Phone: 360.565.6459
ISBN# 978-1-63751-426-9
Library of Congress Control Number
 Book Catalog Info Categories:
   Reference

CadmusPublishing.com

I'll Find You Again – Cornell Hurley Jr.

Dedication

I would like to dedicate this book to someone near and dear to my heart. Someone who took the time to listen when no one else would. This special someone has inspired me to change my life in many ways. She has inspired me to not only change for myself but for her as well. This special someone I cannot name; so I will always hold her within my heart. They say it is crazy what people will do for love but it is even crazier what I have been willing to do for you. If for any reason in the future I cannot be with you and you find yourself thinking of me, then go to your bookshelf and there my love for you will always be. I love you with all of my heart and I can only pray that one day I will find you again. This is for you.

I'll Find You Again – Cornell Hurley Jr.

Prologue

In the summer of 1989, I Shirley Ann Thomas, fell in love with my high school sweetheart, Cornell Hurley. After realizing we were meant to be together, we planned to uphold our commitment we made towards the love we shared. We were to uphold this commitment of ours by planning my pregnancy. On September 6, 1990, I gave birth to our son Cornell Hurley Jr.

From the moment I laid eyes on him I knew he was no ordinary child. At the age of one due to an untimely death Cornell lost his father. The death of his father was a challenge for both he and I. There were many times Cornell had to witness the joy of other children with their fathers, whether it was at the bus stop, school events, and within the comfort of our home. However, with the love of his grandparents, aunts, and uncles Cornell made it through the many troubling times he faced as a child.

Growing up Cornell – as most children his age – wanted nothing more than to play all day long. If ever there was a child in the neighborhood that did not have a friend it was only because they had yet to meet Cornell. He would love everyone he encountered as if he had known them for years, as he still does to this very day. Whenever he would get quiet, I knew that it was time for me to go investigate. Cornell had an undying love for animals such as dogs and snakes. I would often remind him that his inquiring mind would one day cause him grave trouble.

As Cornell grew older he would often speak of finding a woman who would commit to him as he was willing to commit to her. He desperately wanted

I'll Find You Again – Cornell Hurley Jr.

to find a woman who would love him just as much as he loved everyone else. On numerous occasions he would express his need for a loving, affectionate, and understanding woman that would be proud of him and all that he stood to accomplish. Eventually he found exactly what he had been searching for. Unfortunately, just as quick as he had found exactly what he was looking for, he had lost it all just as quick. Before the honeymoon had come to an end, tragedy struck and Cornell was sentenced to twenty-five years in prison.

Right before his eyes everything he had worked for was falling apart. The big question then became, could love withstand the time he would have to serve behind bars. As the days, months, and years went by it became evident that love was not as strong as he dreamed it could be. Cornell began losing close friends, losing contact with certain family members, and eventually losing his wife as well. The only things he had left were a few family members and the joy of being a father to his son, Cornell Hurley III.

During some of the most difficult moments in his life, Cornell still found a way to continue loving others. Since his incarceration, I have had moments when I wanted to give up on myself. Over the last eight years, I have felt as if I was at the end of the road enduring the incarceration of my son. Then out of nowhere I would receive a call or a letter from Cornell, full of encouragement. Although it took a while, by the Grace of God my son has begun pulling his life back together. After placing his faith in Allah he has found a passion for writing.

It is not often a parent can be their child's friend but Cornell and I have become best friends. We listen to one another without passing judgment or as he would say, getting in our feelings. It is a pleasure to be Cornell's mother and I am excited to have had the chance of helping him complete this project. I thank

I'll Find You Again – Cornell Hurley Jr.

God he is staying focused and using his time wisely while inside of the Concrete Jungle. I am his number one fan. Our relationship grows stronger by the day.

The love a mother has for her child is genuine. The love a child has for their mother will never end. It is the kind of love that will withstand a prison sentence. However, the love which Cornell seeks a mother cannot give to her child; she can only pray that he finds what he is looking for. I have no idea who this mystery woman is that my son continues to speak of, but I would like to thank her from the bottom of my heart for allowing my son to feel loved from where he is. Love is beautiful, full of highs and lows. The author has done a great job at expressing the emotions which he felt for his mystery woman, whether they be good or bad. Enjoy!

Shirley Ann Thomas

I'll Find You Again – Cornell Hurley Jr.

Why do fools fall in love? Honestly, I have no idea. I was insane to give love another chance. How stupid I was to fall back in love.

I'll Find You Again – Cornell Hurley Jr.

Stupid Love

Stupid is as stupid does
So stupid we are to fall in love
No answer for all the specifics
So we answer love with all of the above
So if stupid is as stupid does
You must be insane to fall in love
I wasn't stupid but loving you was
Stupid as the situation between you and I was
Somehow we fell deeper in love
Not realizing how stupid it was
If love was meant to heal
Why does it hurt the way it does
I once had a lover try and teach me the way of love
But she didn't know that love is just as stupid
As the one who falls in love
It is what it is
Stupid is as stupid does
So is love

I'll Find You Again – Cornell Hurley Jr.

I am not sorry for doing anything that I did. I only pray that I can have the experience once more: so that I could feel your love again. If you are no longer willing to break the rules at least bend them for us; so that we can be more than friends.

I'll Find You Again – Cornell Hurley Jr.

Unforgiving Sin

I made an unforgiving mistake
Head bowed in prostration
Kissing the ground praising you

I was intrigued by you
From the crown of your head
To the curves of your waist

The forbidden fruit was you
Though Allah may be displeased with me
I could not go on without tasting you

I'll Find You Again – Cornell Hurley Jr.

I have not seen a grasshopper in a while. I have not seen a grasshopper since I found out that you would no longer come around.

I'll Find You Again – Cornell Hurley Jr.

Grasshopper

A lime green critter came and went

With a message I did not quite get

I was told someone special would come around

Leaving no details as in when they would come

When I looked up the critter was gone

So I waited until I could wait no more

With a curious mind and an open heart

I began to explore not traveling far

I was stopped along the way

The day you captured my heart

Important to me you will always be

It is because of you I now believe

That lime green critters will always bring

The most important, amazing, and special things

As it did when it brought you to me

I'll Find You Again – Cornell Hurley Jr.

Before I met you I was afraid that I would never love again. Now I worry that I may love you a little too much. I thought you loved me, I now worry that I was wrong.

I'll Find You Again – Cornell Hurley Jr.

I Worry

I worry what the world may think
How could I have fallen so deep
For someone who fears what I wish for us to be
Worried that if they'd fall for me
They'll be led astray, much closer to me
I worry what the world may see
How is it that I cry for your love
In the comfort of my bed
I chase after you in my sleep
I worry that the world may see, for you I am weak
They will be left wondering
How any of this came to be
I worry what the world may do to us
It may not allow you enough time for me
Casting darkness where there should be light
Taking your sight so that you never reach for me
Without your love I worry
I worry I may not make it
I also worry that the entire world will see
That I worried for nothing at all
Maybe we weren't meant to be
And not once did you worry about me
I'm worried we may never be

I'll Find You Again – Cornell Hurley Jr.

I worry for you, I worry for me

I am as worried as can be

I'll Find You Again – Cornell Hurley Jr.

If you want to go fast go alone, but if you want to go far, go together.

Ancient Proverbs

I'll Find You Again – Cornell Hurley Jr.

Journey

I find joy in traveling this journey blind
I decided to follow my heart neglecting my eyes
Any pain along the way with open arms I will embrace
I would rather love and learn than not have love at all

Falling for you was the easy part
Hitting rock bottom, I shall cherish my beautiful scars
No illusion I am truly in love with who you are
My intention along this journey is to capture your heart
I can't recall where this journey began
My only wish is that it never end
I questioned before the journey began
By the end will you and I be lovers or friends

I'll Find You Again – Cornell Hurley Jr.

It's impossible to count the amount of breaths we take within a day but it's quite simple to count the amount of times we have it taken away. So are the steps towards love.

I'll Find You Again – Cornell Hurley Jr.

Steps Towards Love

The steps I took towards love
For some strange reason I could not feel
Though I plead with my feet to stop
They continued to move at their own will
Closer to love though the ground had no more room to give
Somehow they continued to walk forming their own will
As I came closer your true beauty was revealed
Without the slightest touch I could feel you
As if you stood beneath my heels
My footsteps towards your love have been fossilized in sand
The steps I took towards your love will forever remain
I will always travel back to you

I'll Find You Again – Cornell Hurley Jr.

If only my heart would allow my mind to think for just one moment, then maybe I could move on. You were supposed to be a friend of mine but my heart refused to allow that to be. Turns out you were the girl of my dreams.

I'll Find You Again – Cornell Hurley Jr.

The Heart

The heart runs rapidly
Staying far away from the undeserving
Moving from one to another in a hurry
Never leaving behind troubles nor worries

The heart beats rapidly
With no signs of slowing down
Never missing a single beat
Never changing its sound

The heart can be broken a million times
Only to put itself together again
Turning around and giving itself over and over again
Know that it has the power to mend

The heart knows no defeat
It refuses to accept failure
The heart will continue trying
Until it goes without a sound

Without the beat of its drum
Without its two feet to run
Even without its power to mend

I'll Find You Again – Cornell Hurley Jr.

The heart will never stop

Death is the only thing

That will conquer the heart in the end

I'll Find You Again – Cornell Hurley Jr.

I may not be the best but I can assure you that I am the one; the best you ever had.

I'll Find You Again – Cornell Hurley Jr.

The One

I am not the man your mother wanted to come along

I am not the dream your father had for his princess

But one day you will come to see

That I am the best for you as you are for me

Excuse me for being blunt but fuck your mom and dad

One day they will realize I am the one

I am the best you ever had

I'll Find You Again – Cornell Hurley Jr.

You are a reflection of me. We have both experienced the same pain. We have both made it out of situations that would have crippled most. We are one in the same.

I'll Find You Again – Cornell Hurley Jr.

Opposites Attract

Opposites connect which explains us
The beauty and the beast
Magnetic energy between the west and east
Surely it explains you and me
On days when I shine bright as the sun
You are as dark as the midnight hour
If we somehow end up on the same page
Wandering around hopelessly looking for love
That day will decide our fate
Because I swore the day I met you
My true love I would come alive
Meaning you would pass right by
With me saying hi and you saying bye
Opposites do attract but I wonder why

I'll Find You Again – Cornell Hurley Jr.

Allow me to kiss your scars and caress your pain. With me as your man, you will never hurt again; this I can assure you.

I'll Find You Again – Cornell Hurley Jr.

Shattered Glass

She was so beautifully shattered into pieces
When I met her at an all-time low
But something about her shined brightly
Giving off a dark but heavenly glow
Broken apart by the many lovers she'd trusted before
She bled from her heart and hands
As she began piecing herself together
Promising that she would love no more

In the shattered pieces that remained
I saw our reflection as I stood nearby
In that moment, I knew I could offer more
More than any lover she'd trusted before
For me her promise she broke
So that she could love and trust once more

She finished the puzzle, mending her heart
Open wounds transitioned to blemishes, leaving her memory scarred
No longer broken, she crystallized her heart
Giving it to me, trusting that it would never again fall apart

I'll Find You Again – Cornell Hurley Jr.

Bees never tend to stick around once all of the nectar has run dry. If only you were a fly instead, maybe you would have stuck around through all of my bullshit.

I'll Find You Again – Cornell Hurley Jr.

Bumble Bee

A bumble bee you could be but only for me
A rose that beats rapidly has blossomed inside of me
Buzzing around an unconditional love
Flying throughout my thoughts and dreams
A bumble bee now follows me
Receiving nectar as sweet as honey
Dripping from the rose inside of me
Without the fear of being stung
My queen bee shall forever live inside of me
A precious bumble bee you are to me

I'll Find You Again – Cornell Hurley Jr.

Every word you spoke was full of passion. I miss the sound of your voice and the warmth of each and every word you spoke.

I'll Find You Again – Cornell Hurley Jr.

Shhhh…

When love begins to give its speech
We should all take a moment of silence
Shhhh listen in to the message love has to give
Love has something to say that is original
Secret messages hidden within
Shhhh have patience listen in
Be quiet and give love a chance

I'll Find You Again – Cornell Hurley Jr.

Loving you is like the deep end of the pool, you don't go towards it with intentions of only sticking your toes in.

I'll Find You Again – Cornell Hurley Jr.

Lil Bit

Sure for some it may do
It's just enough to build a lil trust
Keeping the mind satisfied for a lil while
For me it just won't do
I need more than a lil bit
When it comes to you

I'll Find You Again – Cornell Hurley Jr.

Love creates hope in situations where there shouldn't be. You gave me all the hope I will ever need.

I'll Find You Again – Cornell Hurley Jr.

Dreaming of Love

Love has set sail over the horizon never to be seen again
Only those who have experienced love will ever see it again
By remembering what was as if it were a vivid dream
Together we can ensure that love will be seen
Without closing your eyes we can live out our dreams
Showing the world that love is more than just a dream

I'll Find You Again – Cornell Hurley Jr.

The heart knows no limits and will endure the worst of pain. This is how two people who are broken can find each other and somehow love again. Our hearts were meant to do more than beat. Allow your heart to love me.

I'll Find You Again – Cornell Hurley Jr.

It

Let it shatter

Put it back together again

Let it bend

So that it may mend

This time around it will be stronger

Than when what was meant to be forever came to an end

Live, learn, love again

It will be better this time around

Just give it a chance

Your heart is dying to love again

I'll Find You Again – Cornell Hurley Jr.

Teach me how to love you and I will prove to you that I do indeed care for you.

Allow me to prove my love for you is true.

I'll Find You Again – Cornell Hurley Jr.

Prove My Love

Back and forth which way do I go
Truth be told I'm unsure
Whether I should stay or go
You see our relationship is concrete
Like an oak tree to the ground
My roots are connected to your heart
Which won't allow for me to leave
Though I try my best to move around
My mind, my body, my soul
Belongs to no one other than you
You've captured every single part of me
And thrown away the key
I've said all that can possibly be said
I've done all that can be done
Only to find myself wondering around
Thinking of how I could possibly prove my love for you
You see these poems of mine just won't do
Because I am completely out of ideas
But still fighting to prove my love for you
I would lay it all down for you
Turn every friend of mine into an enemy
Just to go to war for you
If you were short of breath

I'll Find You Again – Cornell Hurley Jr.

I'd take my final breath giving it to you
In so many words what I am saying is
I would do anything for you
Just to prove my love is true
With all of this I hope that you see
I haven't been acting crazy
Just doing any and everything
In order to prove my love to you

I'll Find You Again – Cornell Hurley Jr.

I would gladly turn my friends into enemies to wage war for you. So step outside your fortress, knowing that you shall be secure with me.

I'll Find You Again – Cornell Hurley Jr.

7 Steps Away

Life can be fast paced at times
Most people we meet are only passing through
But something special happened when I ran into you
Lost in a world full of sin
In desperate need of a true friend
Placing my feet on solid ground
Solely to stand in your way
Praying you wouldn't pass me by
Now my feet remain planted in place
In memory of that beautiful day

We may not have all the answers
But with just a bit of faith in love
We can conquer the world you and I
We can crawl, walk, run
And one day jump into what was meant to be
I am only asking that you step outside of your box
If not for yourself, then do it for me
Because within these arms true love awaits
I can assure you everything will be okay
All you have to do is take seven steps this way

I'll Find You Again – Cornell Hurley Jr.

I envy the sun because it is clear as day, it has French kissed your beautiful black skin.

I'll Find You Again – Cornell Hurley Jr.

Beautiful Sin

Lewis said his only sin was his beautiful black skin
Dark as the midnight hour, he came out, they went in
I sure wish he could have lived to see you
It would have been a sin for someone not to stare at you
Not because you were dining in
Or riding in the front where most wouldn't dare
But simply because your skin is a grave sin
Causing both men and women to stare
Black and beautiful there is no reason for you to repent
My only prayer is that I get to see you again
In your presence I have not one word to say
I only wish to stare at your skin
Lusting at your outer layer day and night
Is my only sin and I must repent
God forgive me though it may be wrong
I will continue to lust and admire her beautiful skin
I pray the sun sets midday
So that the entire world reflects her skin
Something so beautiful and black should have never been a sin
God did not make it a sin, man did

I'll Find You Again – Cornell Hurley Jr.

I should have known that you were a thief from the start. Before I could fix my lips for a kiss and before I could ever say I love you. You stole my heart, now I have nothing to give.

I'll Find You Again – Cornell Hurley Jr.

Nothing to Give

I can't give you anything but love
That big diamond ring may have to wait
Other than love I have nothing to give
I desperately searched for something free
I attempted to trap the birds and bees
Light as the wind, the finches were too swift
The makers of honey were far from sweet
I hung my head in defeat
Knowing that you deserve the world at your feet
But I have nothing to give

I'll Find You Again – Cornell Hurley Jr.

The fact that I have to keep you as one of my deepest secrets does not bother me. I will always keep you to myself.

I'll Find You Again – Cornell Hurley Jr.

Treasure

One man's trash is another man's treasure

For safekeeping bury your treasure deep

Do not allow it to be on display for all to see

Keep it hidden in the depth of your mind

Although the tongue may wish to speak of what the mind hides

Keep your treasure hidden behind the white of your teeth

You have something of value, something to keep

If one man's trash is another man's treasure to seek

Thank God for the man who did away with you

Now you are my treasure to forever keep

I'll Find You Again – Cornell Hurley Jr.

I only saw what I wanted for us to be. I imagined that we would live out our dreams. I failed to notice the obstacles that stood before us.

I'll Find You Again – Cornell Hurley Jr.

Imagine Time

My imagination made you good
I saw no flaws at all
My imagination made me stay
Although in the back of my mind
I knew a thousand miles away wouldn't be safe
My imagination made me see
Life without you would be horrible for me

In due time you became cold
I saw you for you
With a little more time I realized
Your truth was only a lie
With nothing but time on my side
It was much easier to say goodbye
I imagine in time, I am sure to find
A love that doesn't hide behind beautiful lies

I'll Find You Again – Cornell Hurley Jr.

Love is a virus. A virus which I contracted from you.

I'll Find You Again – Cornell Hurley Jr.

Not Meant To Be

The love between you and I
Was a love not meant to be
The world was not prepared for us
How did we change what was meant to be
Opposites do attract because you and I were not meant to be
An indescribable love formed between you and me
Though we both knew that we weren't meant to be

I'll Find You Again – Cornell Hurley Jr.

I must have apologized a thousand times and would have done so a thousand more, if I had known I was burning your time. We can never get back the burnt time but the memories we will have forever.

I'll Find You Again – Cornell Hurley Jr.

Burning Time

I do not wish to waste your time
It is not your fault, it is all mine
This is not the first time I failed at love
You deserve the world which I cannot give
I could not lie if I tried
There is nothing to say nor write
Not enough words that would rhyme
To tell you for the millionth time
If you truly love me, my love
You are truly wasting your time
Leave me alone, I will be just fine
Let no tears fall from your eyes
I love you too much to allow you to stay
So I will find someone less important
Burning all of their time
Surely the blame will be all mine
I sincerely apologize for burning your time

I'll Find You Again – Cornell Hurley Jr.

Like memories of my hometown, thinking of you always brings me joy. However, I can always go back and visit where I came from but I have no way of finding you. I love you like a small town. Maybe one day after I rise from the mud we can travel back-back and place our feet in the sand or we could travel back to slums of the land where I came from.

I'll Find You Again – Cornell Hurley Jr.

Small Town Love

How could I fall for you
When I'm in love with a small town
When the melting tar of gravel roads
For many years have held me down
While your words were carelessly thrown around
Like trash littering the ground of a small town
For you I will pay the fine
Committing to a lifetime of community service
Caressing the grass while picking up your many lies
That fell upon deaf ears, before hitting the ground
Destroying the beautiful view in a small town

I'll Find You Again – Cornell Hurley Jr.

Sometimes I wish the worst for you. Hurt people hurt people so it's only right that I wish you more pain than you caused me.

I'll Find You Again – Cornell Hurley Jr.

Sleep Tight

The pile of lies on which you lay
Allows for you to sleep throughout the night
While the pain you gave keeps me awake
I hope that the temporary love you gave
No longer comforts you but hunts you when alone at night
Only then will I be able to sleep tight

I'll Find You Again – Cornell Hurley Jr.

We should have fought harder in the name of love.

I'll Find You Again – Cornell Hurley Jr.

Lover's Quarrel

Inside of a lover's quarrel
Back and forth we go
Neither of us willing to quit
Reaching out for what we once had before
A love that is daring and dangerous
Standing toe-to-toe inside the ring
Round after round never allowing for the quarrel to end
What is the point of having love
If it is not worth fighting for
In the name of love let the quarrel begin
After the TKO we will stand
Battered and bruised giving love another chance

I'll Find You Again – Cornell Hurley Jr.

Love is a game either you play or get played. This time around I wish I had played the game but instead I've learned how it feels to be played.

I'll Find You Again – Cornell Hurley Jr.

One Rule

I am obsessed I cannot help but think of you
I am a fool to forget the game I gave to you
There was not much to remember only one rule
Just because you fall in love with someone
Does not mean they will fall for you too
If only I had remembered the number one rule

I'll Find You Again – Cornell Hurley Jr.

Friendship takes fear from the heart

Mahabharata 5-1 BC

I'll Find You Again – Cornell Hurley Jr.

Prideship

This poem hurt my eyes
I wanted to while writing this
But had too much pride to let one slide
To sit before my canvas and cry
Would defiantly do something to my pride
But for you I will attempt to put my pride aside
For you this one last time

How could you run away and hide
I gave you all when I barely had anything to give
When things got hard it was too easy for you to slide
Moving on continuing your life without me on cloud nine
I now feel as if you completely doubted me
All I said I could give and be
I was willing to hand my life over and live for you
So how is it possible that we could just be friends
Being friends was never part of the plan when we began
SO you should know it's not how I would like it to end
I tried pushing my pride aside
However for you I'm emotional, I must give in
So the answer to your question is no
I cannot and will not ever be your friend

I'll Find You Again – Cornell Hurley Jr.

I don't think you realize what your words can do, words of affirmation is all that I ever wanted from you. Know that I am still dying to hear from you.

I'll Find You Again – Cornell Hurley Jr.

Read My Lips

It's not what you do
Rather how you do what you do
It's not what you say
Rather how you say what you say
Read my lips as I say alligator fool
Mimicking the those beautiful words
Knowing you are no fool
Check out my alligator grin
Notice the twinkle in my eye
As I say I love you again

10. There is sickness in their hearts and God only lets their sickness increase. They will suffer a painful punishment for their lies.

2 The Cow

The Clear Quran

I'll Find You Again – Cornell Hurley Jr.

The Heifer

A hypocrite for loving you
My mind says to move on
Maybe find another love similar to you
But I am disdained at the thought of leaving you

My heart is out of shape
In desperate need of mending
Shifting ever so slightly
Back to its original form again

Love is a sickness
That we constantly wallow in
A virus that conquers the mind and heart
Leading us to our final destination
Of heartache and pain once again

I'll Find You Again – Cornell Hurley Jr.

Why couldn't we make time stand still? I was happy with where we stood and would have stayed there forever.

I'll Find You Again – Cornell Hurley Jr.

Nature

We pray for answers which are hard to find
Dropping to our knees praying to the All Mighty divine
For what stands right before our eyes
Here on earth we have certainly died a thousand times
Being resurrected as a sign we will survive

My fingers went numb not feeling a thing
My eyes began to water at the molesting chill
Looking towards evergreen trees nature surely sent as a sign
Although they did not shed a single leaf
They could no longer stay green
For some strange reason against their will
From within what was rich and green, mahogany now bleeds
Just like the seasons in time all shall change
I should have been attentive to you like I was to nature
Before thinking that you would stay the same

I'll Find You Again – Cornell Hurley Jr.

You taught me to never look back. Either they could not keep up with your progress or it simply was not meant to be. Sometimes we outgrow one another. Fuck it; it is what it is.

I'll Find You Again – Cornell Hurley Jr.

Jaded

I have been stabbed so many times
My heart cannot help but bleed out
Caught in the same trap again and again
I swear I will never make it out
If there was a lesson to be learned
For some strange reason I fear I may never get it

Now if love was a bout
I have went toe-to-toe, blow for blow
Muhammad Ali rope and dope
Put love in a choke hold vowing to never let it go
But your love was stubborn so I decided to let it go
Love and me we just can't seem to get along
Whenever we link there is no peace
Call me jaded if you wish
But remember you heard it from me
Love is just a dream full of false hope
It is never what it seems to be

I'll Find You Again – Cornell Hurley Jr.

You just like talking huh? Keeping the truth to yourself knowing that it would expose the truth, revealing that you hurt just like everyone else. Stop lying to yourself!

I'll Find You Again – Cornell Hurley Jr.

Lying Ass

You didn't want to fall in love
You just heard about how good love was
You figured if they had it then so could you
You had nothing to offer at all
You were willing to take but give none at all
You were good at extracting the truth
Although you never told the truth at all
You are nothing more than a dirty dog

I'll Find You Again – Cornell Hurley Jr.

How does it feel to be all that someone needs? Because that's what you were to me. I want to know exactly how it feels...

I'll Find You Again – Cornell Hurley Jr.

How It Feels

I would not mind trading places with you
Because I am dying to know how it feels
To feel something I have never felt before
After acknowledging your flaws
To have someone cherish you as if perfect
How does it feel to be number one overall
No longer having to pretend at all
Being loved for simply being you
I don't know how it feels at all

I'll Find You Again – Cornell Hurley Jr.

I miss your touch and I will never forget what it felt like.

I'll Find You Again – Cornell Hurley Jr.

Feel Good

It felt like a teenager behind the wheel for the first time
On an open road with nothing but freedom and time
That's what it felt like

It felt like a never ending overseas flight
We continued to ascend with no lows
We were in control of our destination
That's what it felt like

It felt like the butterfly effect
We went in not knowing who we were
We came out even more confused than when we went in
However after acquiring our wings we were a sight to see
That's what it felt like

We were raging war for a good cause
Our mission was to reach the pinnacle of love
We swore that we would never give up
Somehow on the battlefield you were injured by love
Now all I have is memories of us
But that's what it felt like when I had your love

I'll Find You Again – Cornell Hurley Jr.

I desperately tried but could never find the words to describe you. You are you and that's the only way that I could possibly pay homage to my love. Nothing or no one else could ever compare to you. Lord knows I love me some you!

I'll Find You Again – Cornell Hurley Jr.

You

You are you

And that's special to me

You are a poem

Worth reading from beginning to end

You are a song on repeat

Which I will listen to again

You are beautiful

Both inside and out

You are a whisper

With great volumes of love

You are you

And no one compares

You are you and that's why I care

You are my all in all

You mean the world to me

I'll Find You Again – Cornell Hurley Jr.

What I wanted form you was not an ideal but that is what made our relationship special. I wanted to change the narrative, change people's mind about what could be.

I'll Find You Again – Cornell Hurley Jr.

Change Pt. 2

Even the leaves grow old and fall
Summer days go dim bringing forth a chill
Beautiful bundles of joy grow grey and old
The only thing constant is change
So love me for who I am
But surely that too shall change

Our beautiful memories will become old
Touching the back of our minds and fading away
Although you say that you love me
Love never lasts long this we knew
Change will come forcing you to move along
Until that day comes I will patiently wait
Change as we know will surely come
Change will most definitely take you away from me
Change is the only thing that will remain constant
For some strange reason I thought you would stay

I'll Find You Again – Cornell Hurley Jr.

Adam and Eve is only a reflection of what you and I were meant to be.

I'll Find You Again – Cornell Hurley Jr.

Jinn Love

I was supposed to be your Adam
You were meant to be my Eve
Together in the Garden of Eden we'd forever be
You said you loved me with all of your heart
When you did not yet know the meaning of love
Beyond death my love would have followed you
Heaven or hell wherever you went my love
I would have surely followed you
If I could I would again and again
Every bite would taste just as sweet
A life full of passion and sin
Was made for you and I until the end

I'll Find You Again – Cornell Hurley Jr.

You should have tried a little harder than you did. Giving up should not have been an option.

I'll Find You Again – Cornell Hurley Jr.

This and That

I tried crying until my eyes went dry
Which only left my pillow soaking wet

I tried shot after shot attempted suicide
Only to find you still on my mind

I tried talking to my ex
But it had little to no affect

I tried a little bit of this and that
The fact still remains the same you're gone

I'll Find You Again – Cornell Hurley Jr.

Allah has blessed me with a genuine love. A love that only she can give.

I'll Find You Again – Cornell Hurley Jr.

Bloody Knees

My blood stained knees are proof
That I plead and I pray
Begging for sympathy and forgiveness
For the many lies I have told
From my convictions I pray I will be freed
Down on bending knees until they bleed
Asking God that He give you to me
I won't be long this time around
Being that there is only one thing I need
I continue to pray though my knees bleed
Begging God, give her to me please

I'll Find You Again – Cornell Hurley Jr.

When I could no longer express the way I feel for you, the tears began to flow.

I'll Find You Again – Cornell Hurley Jr.

Cry For You

I cry for you

Because your story compels me to

Because of all you've been through

I cry for you

Because of what you had to endure

Because of the damage I caused you

I cry for you

Because I sincerely care for you

Because no woman could ever compare to you

I cry for you

Because I fear we cannot be

Because of the many barriers between you and me

I cry for you

With a smile on my face

A gaping hole in my heart

Tears that I cry for you symbolize

Nothing will ever keep us apart

I cry for you

I'll Find You Again – Cornell Hurley Jr.

How selfish of me to ask for the best of you, knowing that she deserves nothing less than what I've asked of you. So if possible can you give me whatever is left of you?

I'll Find You Again – Cornell Hurley Jr.

Baby Girl

I may not know enough about you
At this point to call you mine
I may not have been in the picture long enough
To want a Kodak moment with you in it
However, I am in love with your mother
And I intend to stay around
My intentions are to never hurt you
Like the vow I made to your mother
I will never let you down
You see the difference between him and I
Is that I want to be around
I truly believe that being in your life
Will be worth it if only to see you smile
Talk to me about anything you'd like
I will manage to keep the bad ones away
If you would like to walk the straight path
Down the aisle with a ring arm in arm
I will gladly lead the way
Without a bat in hand I will step up to the plate
Fulfilling my role as a step dad
Until the day I must give you away
Baby girl know that with me
You and your mother will always be safe

I'll Find You Again – Cornell Hurley Jr.

No one could ever define what we shared. We set the standard for what love was.

I'll Find You Again – Cornell Hurley Jr.

Love Defined

Our love has been defined in such a way
No lexicon could find the words to explain
Philosophers could not find proper words to say
About the unique love we've made

Written in ink our love still cannot be defined
A love so divine cannot be seen upon lines
As our hearts bleed for one another
The definition of our love becomes blurred between lines

You allowed our love to be defined
By an unknown amount of time, barbwire, and conflicting minds
Our love is still considered divine
With the remainder of twenty-five and patience on our side
You will find the love we had still cannot be defined

So what is love
Explain to me what I cannot have
Because your definition of love reads differently from mine
Truly I wish we had a love that could not be defined
Let's come together and redefine, one last time
This will surely take forever because I assure you
Our love cannot be defined

I'll Find You Again – Cornell Hurley Jr.

I need you to hold on to me...

I'll Find You Again – Cornell Hurley Jr.

Grip Tight

Reaching out for a hand to hold
Simply wanting someone to be there
Anyone who would care to listen or try to understand
Unfortunately you realized too late
The hand that you have been reaching for
No longer reaches out to grasp for those wanting love
Now you are left to stand alone
Holding on tightly to the agonizing pain still wanting love

I'll Find You Again – Cornell Hurley Jr.

No matter how high I will climb, towering heights for you.

I'll Find You Again – Cornell Hurley Jr.

Fences

Whoever built fences meant to be cruel
White picket fences straight as pearly white teeth a sight to see
Stone walls hide treasure thieves desperately seek
Mesh fences which have had their diamonds plucked
Leaving gaping holes for the incarcerated to peek
Diamond mesh fences stand to remind me
There will always be a divider between you and I

I'll Find You Again – Cornell Hurley Jr.

To be released from prison within the month of September wouldn't be a gift unless I was released to you. Behind confining walls I have patiently waited for years but for you I can no longer wait. I just pray that you can wait for me.

I'll Find You Again – Cornell Hurley Jr.

September 6

I'll be gone until September

Let's pick up where we left off

Make new memories ones we can remember

Better than the one where we left off

You and I we got so much to do

Plans formed behind confining walls

Fairytales turned into reality is what I have planned for you

Together we will travel the world

Touching the seven seas

Dressed in the best linen

Eating the finest cuisine

Exploring every country

Until we find the perfect place to stay

But know that I will be gone until September

I pray that you can wait

Because this is what our future holds

With patience I will wait as the months unfold

If we shall have to wait beyond September

For you on the inside of these confining walls I will cry

As the days, months, and years pass us by

I'll Find You Again – Cornell Hurley Jr.

Without you I am nothing, please don't leave.

I'll Find You Again – Cornell Hurley Jr.

Pretty Baby

So pretty you are
Breaking me down to my knees
Pretty as the birds dancing through autumn leaves
Pretty my love do me a favor and never leave
If you tried on hands and knees I'd plead
Begging you pretty don't leave
You'd be the one to make me beg
I might hold out and pout instead
You won't give in, okay then you win
Pretty baby let's not scream and shout
If you would just listen for a second
Maybe we could work this out
Hold me close because I refuse to back out
I will make it right so you won't have to leave
With my pride aside I will beg and plead
Pretty baby, pretty please don't leave

I'll Find You Again – Cornell Hurley Jr.

The story I have nobody can steal.
Dough Williams, 1989

I'll Find You Again – Cornell Hurley Jr.

Your Story

This is your story to tell
You are in control of the narrative
You hold the key to all possibilities
Write me in I will act accordingly
The script will be mine to live
Cast me for the role and my all I will give
This is your story to tell
Just don't forget to write me in

I'll Find You Again – Cornell Hurley Jr.

My secrets will remain safe with you; I have no doubt about it. I trust you enough to tell you anything.

I'll Find You Again – Cornell Hurley Jr.

Snitch

I told as well but not like you
Even if we weren't meant to be
How we grew and the love we shared
Was to leave behind a positive legacy
I showed you my demons, gave you all of my secrets
Those things I exposed for free
The world was to never know the truth
Everything was to rest securely with you
You should have lied instead of telling the truth
I always knew I'd be exposed
I just never thought that it would be by you

I'll Find You Again – Cornell Hurley Jr.

I wish that you'd come back.

I'll Find You Again – Cornell Hurley Jr.

Left Alone

You started this journey with me
Now I must finish all alone
Call me crazy for feeling this way
But it was you who left me all alone
Now that you are further away
My feelings for you have grown
You will never know the pain of walking miles alone
Being in love with someone yet all alone
Starting a journey with your soul mate
Knowing that you will have to finish all alone

I'll Find You Again – Cornell Hurley Jr.

The pain I feel from not accepting what's real and constantly thinking of what could be is driving me insane.

I'll Find You Again – Cornell Hurley Jr.

Insane Window Pain

Instead of pulling me down
Gravity seems to be pulling me forward
Everything that passes my window
I find it hard to ignore
Though I walk backwards my eyes remain forward
I am afraid of what I may miss
Never did I imagine it would come to this
With my eyes bloodshot and strained
At my window in search of you I remain
Since I began looking for you
I have yet to miss a sunrise
The longer I wait, the more pain I feel
I will never give up hope
I will see you again, I swear I will
Even if the glass before me must shatter
In the end my love I will find you again

I'll Find You Again – Cornell Hurley Jr.

It's hard living without you. I want so bad to fall in love again but I would rather not have love, if I can't have you.

I'll Find You Again – Cornell Hurley Jr.

Living

Without you I am simply getting by

My heart beats but the blood has ran dry

My mind wonders where you are

But is now incapable of wondering why

Without you I am simply getting by

My eyes ache without tears to cry

Butterflies avoid my churning stomach

The nectar inside is now bitter sweet

Of course you of all people should know why

Because without you I am not living

I am simply just getting by

I'll Find You Again — Cornell Hurley Jr.

As the distance between you and I continues to grow pushing you further away, my love for you continues to grow. A distant lover I never imagined you to be.

I'll Find You Again – Cornell Hurley Jr.

Get Away

Far away is not far enough for us
Another world or planet is still too close for us
A thousand miles away could not create enough distance between us
How about I run away and you run away too
Creating a greater distance between us two
No matter how far away we go the distance seems to shrink
As I always find my way back to you
Maybe death will do justice
But even then my spirit will be with you
There is no such thing as a distance between us
It doesn't matter where you go my love
I could never get away from you

I'll Find You Again – Cornell Hurley Jr.

What am I to do when my emotions get the best of me and I cannot think clearly?

I'll Find You Again – Cornell Hurley Jr.

I Would Be Wrong

For some reason I cannot hate you
I love you way too much to resent you
My heart tells me to say goodbye
Whenever I attempt to turn around I die inside
The problem is I still love you and you're gone
I want to hate you so bad for giving up what we had
But I would be wrong

I'll Find You Again – Cornell Hurley Jr.

I find it impossible to be that you could no longer be interested in what we could be. I think about you all the time. In order for you to have escaped feeling that was so strong, you had to forget about me.

I'll Find You Again – Cornell Hurley Jr.

Forgotten

I feel like you forgot
You forgot about me
You forgot about all the things we aspired to be
You said I could possibly be
That time was a nonfactor
That you were in no rush to find love
As if you'd secured a spot in your heart for me
I never had to tell you
That you were the one for me
Your sole purpose in life was to be with me
Somehow time and space came between us
Which caused you to forget about me
About the look in my eyes when I said I love you
How could it be my love
I never thought you'd forget about me
Miraculously somehow you forgot how to be
The woman I knew you to be
I never thought the day would come
That my love would forget about me

I'll Find You Again – Cornell Hurley Jr.

I pray you never forget what I wanted for us to be. Most importantly I hope you remember me.

I'll Find You Again – Cornell Hurley Jr.

Remember Me

Remember me as I am
Believe not the stories which are told
Twisted lies become fairytales of the unwise

Remember me as the man I tried to be
Not the man who surfaced in difficult times
But the teddy bear that was hidden inside

Remember me as that fly guy
The friend always making you smile
Giving you all of me hoping our connection would survive

Remember me always thinking of you
No matter how far away you go
I will always be thinking of you

So please remember me

I'll Find You Again – Cornell Hurley Jr.

If I must stay caged in order to receive your love, then forever here I'll stay.

I'll Find You Again – Cornell Hurley Jr.

Here I'll Stay

I was hoping that you would meet me
In a place where love lasted forever and a day
You must have gotten lost along the way
I've been waiting and will continue to wait
Until you arrive here I'll stay

I'll Find You Again – Cornell Hurley Jr.

How could you spoil me rotten by giving me your love and then taking it back?

I'll Find You Again – Cornell Hurley Jr.

Take It

You took my time pressing rewind
Playing with my patience knowing that I hate to wait

You took my mind, scrambled my thoughts
Causing me to imagine the impossible

You took my eyes making me see
There is more to life than me loving only me

You forgot to take the most important things
My heart, my ring, and my last name

I'll Find You Again – Cornell Hurley Jr.

I should have when I had the chance, now I may never know what it feels like.

I'll Find You Again – Cornell Hurley Jr.

Kisses

Muah

I love the taste of your lips

In between vanilla ice cream and a strawberry shake

Is how I would describe the taste

I love kissing all over your face

Muah

With my lips I will erase

Every scar and every blemish

The best kisses I will save

Placing them in a special place

Kissing lips that can't kiss back

Muah Muah Muah

I love kissing you in every way

Dark chocolate kisses I love to taste

Your kisses are the sweetest I ever had

I would still kiss you even if you told me

To pucker up and kiss your ass

I'll Find You Again – Cornell Hurley Jr.

Anything that ever went wrong blame it on me. It is my fault that I could not be who you needed me to be. One day you will see how much I've changed; not only for myself but for you as well.

I'll Find You Again – Cornell Hurley Jr.

Blame Me

Do not blame yourself place it all on me
I could not be there when you needed me
I went away to find a little more of myself
To see if I could be the man you needed me to be
Spending a little too much time away thinking of only me
Not once thinking of how you were doing without me
It hurts to see love fading away right before my eyes
Do not blame yourself blame me
I ruined what could have been between you and I
So do not blame yourself, do not blame love
It is safe to point the finger at me
It is all my fault blame me

I'll Find You Again – Cornell Hurley Jr.

What else is there to say? When you've already said enough.

I'll Find You Again – Cornell Hurley Jr.

Dot Dot Dot

I've written so many
I wish to write no more
I've allowed myself to fall way too deep
Now I wish to explore no more
The spring that flow from my pen
Have run dry not leaving a drop behind
With all that we have written and said
If nothing comes of this
At least this time for once
I can say I gave it a fair try
And if I never find you again
This is the end of my love letter
My love for you has not run dry
But my pen has no more ink to give

...

I'll Find You Again – Cornell Hurley Jr.

Love gives you life, then snatches your heart out of your chest. Without love you wouldn't be and with love you're soon to meet your demise.

I'll Find You Again – Cornell Hurley Jr.

Written Homicide

With the deepest paper cut
I attempted to commit suicide
My eyes began to create a storm
Leaving puddles blurring blue lines
With every stroke of the pen
My wrist began to slit a little more
However, I could not stop scribing for your love
The more I wrote the pain I began to enjoy
If you are reading this poem you won't ever hear from me again
To express my love in words for you brought me to the end
I committed written suicide to express what was held within

I'll Find You Again – Cornell Hurley Jr.

Trust Me

By: Shirly Ann Thomas

Just take my word
Take the words form my mouth
Combine them with the love in your heart
This will allow us to stand

As we are many miles apart
Allow my words alone to be enough
Fight for me
Fight for us
With all of your might

Oh my love be patient
Oh my love be brave for me
Let the Lord work it out
He is my strength, He is my redeemer
His will shall be done

Trust every word I say to you
Trust the actions of my heart
At the moment we stand apart
With only a little time in our way
Be brave, be still

I'll Find You Again – Cornell Hurley Jr.

We won't always be apart

You just have to trust me

I'll Find You Again – Cornell Hurley Jr.

Blessed

By: Raven Johnson

The way we forget

The intensity of the struggles

Making unbreakable promises and covenants

Hoping they will bind us together

While inside we are suffering for one another

I told God I would never love again

Here I am pouring my heart out to another

As he spills his love into me

How easily we forget the tears

The wrenching break

The unexplainable pain

The pain we refuse to bring before God

The pain we thought would never end

Thank God for allowing me to forget

How beautiful to be a woman

A woman who knows no hurt

Having the ability to continue to grow

In a never-ending field of wildflowers

Where pain used to grow but exists no more

I'll Find You Again – Cornell Hurley Jr.

The things I would do if I were to remember

The things I would do to never feel it again

I thank God

For the blessing

Allowing me to always start over again

I'll Find You Again – Cornell Hurley Jr.

Image of Love

By: KaNeisha Thomas

What does love look like

I have seen a few different views

The views are not quite right

It is fair to say I learned from the best

I am expressing self-love

Love me unconditionally

Suppose I gave and gave but never received

Short-changing myself is all I would know

Love is how you look at it

Love is understanding

When nothing else makes sense

Instead of taking a few steps going the extra mile

If I live in the image of love

It would be a forever smile

Love is an image with more to create

Love is an empty canvas allowing for a clean slate

I had the wrong idea of what love was

Until I created my own image of what it was

I'll Find You Again – Cornell Hurley Jr.

Love is to love yourself first
To know who you are
To know what you want to be

If I decide to love
Sharing my life with someone else
They would have to know the ultimate love
The man up above, the perfect image of love
That is how I want it to be

God, myself, and someone there loving me

I'll Find You Again – Cornell Hurley Jr.

More Love More Hope
By: KaNeisha Thomas

Love and hope make for a beautiful combination
In the process of moving forward
They are both the inspiration of motivation
Love yourself because self-love is real
It is a love that no one can steal
Have more love for self do not forget you
Do not leave yourself by the wayside
Do not allow the depths of false love to overtake you
Push through with more love and more hope
This is something you should do for you

I'll Find You Again – Cornell Hurley Jr.

Forgotten Father

By: Shaquille Craig

My heart no longer beats the same
Invisible barriers caused physical pain
Your tiny hand I still dream to hold
Crying at night so nobody knows
My memory fading in your head I can feel
I'm so far away but in my heart you're still near
When I left I was hurt, you were still just a toddler
Please don't let me be another forgotten father

I'll Find You Again – Cornell Hurley Jr.

Dear 7,

    If I could touch you again, I would touch you unlike I have ever touched anyone before. If only I could stand before you once more, I would kiss your most delicate spots savoring the natural flavor. If only I could make you feel the feeling which you have bestowed upon me, you would be mine. How many can truly say that they know what love is? If any I am one, you taught me what love is as well as what love was not. If I never find you again, maybe in another lifetime you will be mine. I pray with this book I have cleared up any doubt that may have lingered in the back of your mind. It was never meant to be a temporary situation, at least on my end. I wanted you to forever be mine. I am in love with who you are not the person you could possibly be. If I never find you again on my heart there will forever be a permanent scar.

                                From the bottom of my heart,
                                      Cornell Hurley Jr.

I'll Find You Again – Cornell Hurley Jr.

www.ingramcontent.com/pod-product-compliance
Lightning Source LLC
Chambersburg PA
CBHW052145070526
44585CB00017B/1981